OBOL HOUSE
PUBLISHING COMPANY

An imprint of Huntsville Independent Press

2112 Morningside Drive NW, Huntsville, AL, 35810

This book is a work of original authorship. It reflects the author's experiences, ideas, research, or imagination, depending on the nature of the content. In some cases, names, identifying details, or circumstances may have been altered for clarity or privacy. The views expressed are those of the author and do not necessarily represent those of the publisher.

Text copyright © 2025 by Cassie Shropshire

All rights reserved, including the right of reproduction in whole or in part in any form. For information about special discounts for bulk purchases, or licensing information, please contact Obol House Publishing Company at +1 (256) 678-0411 or Editor@ObolHouse.com.

Obol House can bring authors to your live event. For more information or to book an event, contact Obol House Publishing Company at +1 (256) 678-0411 or visit our website at: www.ObolHouse.com

Cover design by Cassie Shropshire

Interior design by Cassie Shropshire

The text for this book was set in Bobby Jones.

Manufactured in the United States of America
First Obol House paperback edition November 2025

12345678910

The Library of Congress has cataloged the hardcover edition as follows:

Names: Cassie Shropshire, author.

Title: Save It For Therapy

Identifiers: 979-8-9927321-7-7 (HCV)

THIS WORKBOOK BELONGS TO:

_____

IF FOUND, PLEASE BE A KIND HUMAN AND RESPECT MY PRIVACY BY NOT READING.

MY PHONE NUMBER IS: (   )   -

CALL OR TEXT IF FOUND. YOU'RE THE BEST! THANK YOU!

SAVE IT FOR THERAPY

HEY BEAUTIFUL SOUL!

IF YOU'RE READING THIS, IT MEANS YOU'RE EITHER CONSIDERING THERAPY OR ALREADY ON YOUR THERAPEUTIC JOURNEY, AND YOU WANT TO USE THIS HANDBOOK TO STAY ORGANIZED AND ACCOUNTABLE. I'M SO PROUD OF YOU FOR TAKING THIS STEP! YOUR MENTAL HEALTH IS INCREDIBLY IMPORTANT, AND MY HEART SMILES KNOWING THAT YOU VALUE IT.

THANK YOU FOR YOUR SUPPORT! FEEL FREE TO SHARE YOUR THOUGHTS ABOUT THIS RESOURCE WITH ME AT INFO@SAVEIT4THERAPY.COM.

WITH SO MUCH LOVE,
-CASSIE NICOLE

THERAPY 101

WHAT IS THERAPY?

Therapy, also known as counseling or psychotherapy, is a process where you work with a trained professional to explore your thoughts, feelings, and behaviors in a safe and supportive environment. Its purpose is to help you understand yourself better, manage challenges, and work toward personal growth and emotional well-being.

WHO IS THERAPY FOR?

Mental health does not discriminate. Regardless of your race, ethnicity, gender identity, or religious views, anyone who needs support can benefit from therapy. Therapy is for anyone seeking support, whether you're facing a specific challenge like anxiety, grief, or relationship issues, or simply want to enhance your self-awareness and overall mental health. Therapy is not limited to those in crisis—it's a tool for anyone looking to grow and improve their quality of life.

HOW DO I FIND A THERAPIST?

Finding the right therapist can take time, but it's worth the effort. Start by identifying what you're looking for, such as a therapist who specializes in specific issues or offers a particular approach, like cognitive-behavioral therapy or trauma-informed care. You can search through online directories, ask for recommendations, or consult with your insurance provider for covered options. It's important to choose someone you feel comfortable with, as the connection between you and your therapist is key to success.

THERAPY 101

Therapy is more than just a place to talk—it's a powerful tool for personal growth, healing, and self-discovery. Life can bring challenges that feel overwhelming, emotions that seem unmanageable, or situations where you're unsure how to move forward. Therapy provides a safe, supportive space to explore those experiences, develop healthier ways of thinking and coping, and create meaningful change in your life.

This guide is designed to help you navigate the therapy process with confidence. Whether you're new to therapy or just curious about how it works, this workbook will provide clarity, answer your questions, and empower you to take that first step toward becoming your best self. Remember, seeking help is a sign of strength, and you deserve the support to thrive.

IN THE FOLLOWING PAGES, YOU'LL LEARN ABOUT:

- **The Therapy Process:** What happens in a session? How do you know therapy is working?
- **The Therapist:** Their qualifications, approach, and how to know if they're the right fit for you.
- **Practical Matters:** Costs, insurance, scheduling, and other logistical concerns.
- **Common Concerns:** What if I don't know where to start? Is it normal to feel nervous or emotional?
- **Goals and Outcomes:** How therapy helps and what kind of changes you can expect.

THERAPY 101
THE THERAPY PROCESS

WHAT HAPPENS IN A TYPICAL THERAPY SESSION?
In a typical session, you'll talk about your thoughts, feelings, and experiences. The therapist may ask questions, offer insights, and help you explore challenges. Sessions are a safe space for you to share openly and work toward your goals.

HOW LONG WILL I NEED TO BE IN THERAPY?
This varies depending on your goals and needs. Some people attend for a few months, while others find long-term therapy beneficial. You and your therapist can revisit this as you progress.

WHAT SHOULD I TALK ABOUT IN THERAPY?
Anything that's on your mind—your challenges, emotions, experiences, or even uncertainties about what to share. Therapy is about what feels most important to you.

IS EVERYTHING I SAY CONFIDENTIAL?
Yes, most of what you share is confidential. However, therapists are required by law to report if there's a risk of harm to yourself or others or if child or elder abuse is disclosed.

HOW DO I KNOW IF THERAPY IS WORKING FOR ME?
You may notice changes in your thinking, emotions, or behavior, like feeling more hopeful, managing stress better, or gaining new insights. Regularly discussing progress with your therapist can also help.

THERAPY 101
ABOUT THE THERAPIST

WHAT'S YOUR APPROACH TO THERAPY?
Therapists may use different methods, such as cognitive-behavioral therapy, talk therapy, or mindfulness. They'll usually explain their approach and how it can help with your goals.

DO YOU SPECIALIZE IN ISSUES LIKE MINE?
Therapists often specialize in areas like anxiety, depression, trauma, or relationships. You can ask directly about their experience with your specific concerns.

WHAT QUALIFICATIONS OR TRAINING DO YOU HAVE?
Therapists hold advanced degrees (e.g., Master's or PhD) and have licenses to practice. They also complete ongoing education and training to maintain their credentials.

WILL YOU JUDGE ME OR MY EXPERIENCES?
No. A therapist's role is to support, not judge. They provide a safe, compassionate space for you to share and grow.

HOW DO I KNOW IF YOU'RE THE RIGHT THERAPIST FOR ME?
You should feel comfortable, heard, and supported. If you don't feel a connection after a few sessions, it's okay to discuss it or seek another therapist.

THERAPY 101
PRACTICAL MATTERS

HOW MUCH DOES THERAPY COST, AND IS IT COVERED BY INSURANCE?
Costs vary. Some therapists accept insurance, while others offer sliding-scale fees based on income. It's best to ask your therapist directly or check with your insurance provider.

DO YOU OFFER VIRTUAL SESSIONS?
Many therapists offer online sessions through secure platforms. This can be a convenient option if you prefer or need flexibility.

HOW OFTEN DO I NEED TO COME TO THERAPY?
Most people start with weekly or bi-weekly sessions, but this can change over time. Your therapist will help you decide what works best for your needs.

WHAT HAPPENS IF I NEED TO CANCEL A SESSION?
Therapists usually have a cancellation policy, such as requiring 24-48 hours' notice. Ask your therapist about their specific policy.

WHAT SHOULD I BRING OR PREPARE FOR MY FIRST SESSION?
Just yourself! If you have specific goals or questions, you can bring a notepad to write things down, but it's not required.

THERAPY 101
YOUR CONCERNS

WHAT IF I DON'T KNOW WHAT'S WRONG OR WHERE TO START?
That's okay. Many people feel this way. Your therapist will help you explore your thoughts and feelings to identify what's most important to you.

WHAT IF I GET EMOTIONAL OR CRY DURING A SESSION?
It's completely normal and even therapeutic. Sessions are a safe space to express emotions without judgment.

WILL TALKING ABOUT MY PROBLEMS MAKE THEM WORSE?
While it can be hard at first, exploring your challenges in therapy often leads to relief, understanding, and growth over time.

HOW DO I TALK ABOUT THINGS I'M ASHAMED OR SCARED OF?
Start small and share only what you're comfortable with. Building trust with your therapist can make it easier over time.

WHAT IF I DON'T FEEL COMFORTABLE OPENING UP RIGHT AWAY?
That's perfectly fine. Therapy is a process, and it's normal to take time to build trust and feel ready to share.

THERAPY 101
GOALS AND OUTCOMES

HOW CAN THERAPY HELP ME WITH MY SPECIFIC ISSUES?
Your therapist will tailor sessions to your needs, offering tools, strategies, and insights to address your challenges and help you grow.

CAN THERAPY HELP ME FEEL LESS ANXIOUS OR DEPRESSED?
Yes, therapy can provide coping strategies, emotional support, and tools to help manage and reduce symptoms of anxiety or depression.

WHAT KIND OF CHANGES SHOULD I EXPECT TO SEE OVER TIME?
You might feel more self-aware, manage emotions better, improve relationships, or find clarity in your goals.

WILL YOU GIVE ME ADVICE OR TELL ME WHAT TO DO?
Therapists guide you to find your own answers rather than giving direct advice. They support your decision-making process.

WHAT HAPPENS IF THERAPY DOESN'T SEEM TO BE HELPING?
Talk openly with your therapist about your concerns. They may adjust their approach, or you might decide to explore other options or therapists.

REASONS TO START THERAPY

- You want help with managing your mood
- You want to learn how to manage your anxiety
- You want to develop stress management tools
- You want assistance with adjusting to new life transitions
- You want help processing grief and loss
- You want assistance with career exploration
- You want to increase your confidence and decision-making skills
- You want support with family issues, such as dysfunctional family dynamics or setting boundaries with your family
- You want to improve your relationships and learn how to communicate better

WHY ARE YOU CHOOSING TO START THERAPY?

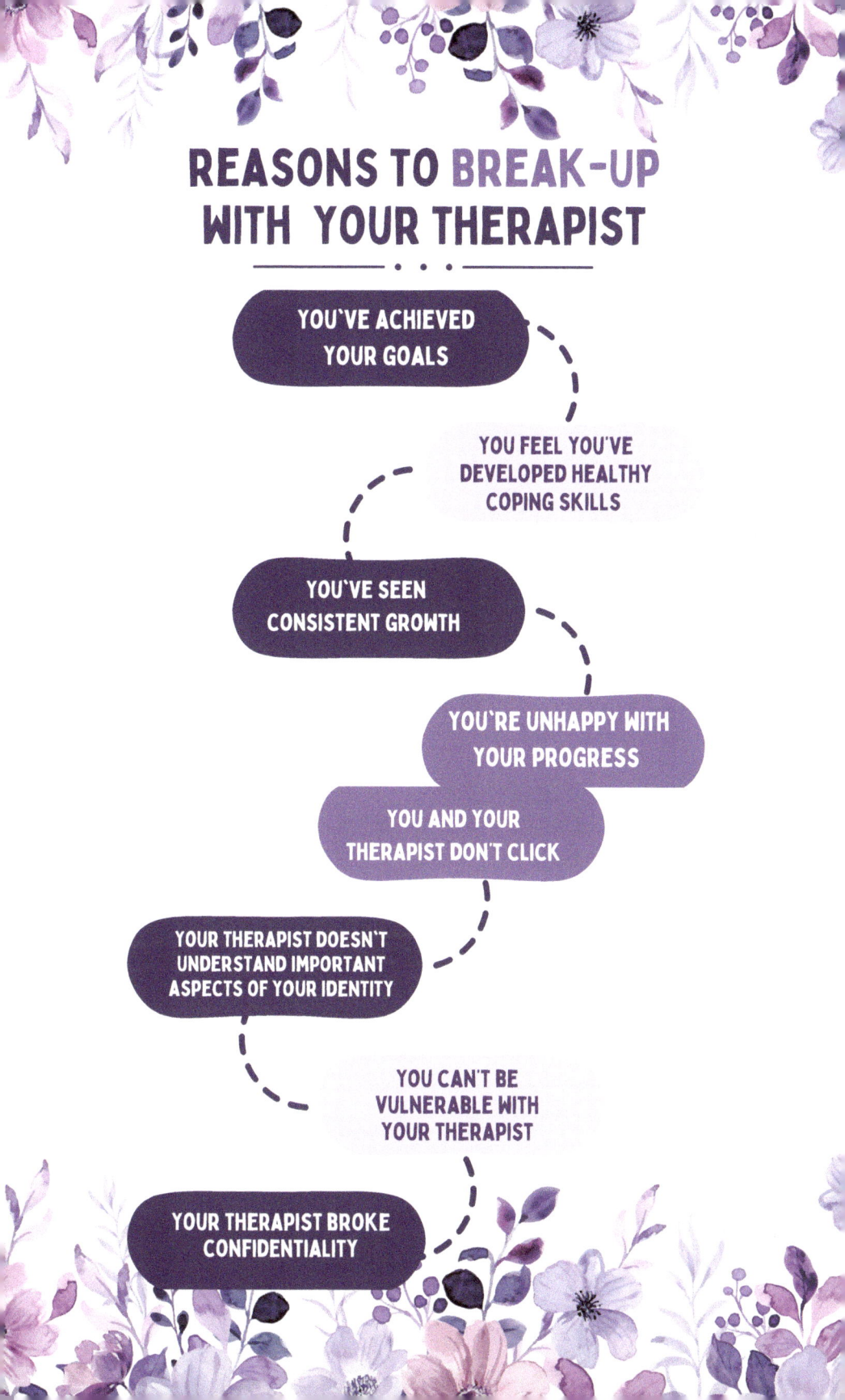

HOW TO BREAK-UP WITH YOUR THERAPIST

1. REFLECT ON YOUR DECISION
Before making any moves, take time to reflect on why you feel it's time to end your therapeutic relationship. It's helpful to know the why behind your decision so you can communicate it clearly.

2. ACKNOWLEDGE YOUR PROGRESS
Recognize the work you've done with your therapist. Even if you feel it's time to part ways, it's important to acknowledge any progress you've made in therapy. This shows respect for the work both you and your therapist have put into your sessions.

3. SCHEDULE A CLOSING SESSION (IF NECESSARY)
If possible, schedule one final session to discuss your decision. This will allow you to process your feelings and create closure. It also gives your therapist a chance to ask any final questions about your decision and offer support during the transition.

4. BE HONEST AND DIRECT
When you speak to your therapist, be honest but kind. Let them know why you're choosing to end the relationship, whether it's due to a lack of connection, wanting a different therapeutic style, or any other reason. Remember, therapy is a safe space, and your therapist is trained to handle this conversation professionally.

> "I've really appreciated the work we've done together, but after thinking it over, I believe it's time for me to take a break from therapy or seek a different therapist. I feel that my needs might be better met elsewhere, and I want to explore that option."

HOW TO BREAK-UP WITH YOUR THERAPIST

5. DISCUSS NEXT STEPS
If you're open to continuing therapy with a different therapist, ask for recommendations. Your current therapist may have suggestions or referrals to help you find a good fit. If you plan on taking a break from therapy, discuss how to transition in a way that feels comfortable to you.

6. THANK THEM FOR THEIR HELP
Ending the relationship on a positive note can be incredibly powerful. Even if things didn't go perfectly, thank your therapist for their support and the work they've done with you. This gratitude helps ensure a respectful and understanding conclusion.

7. REVIEW ADMINISTRATIVE DETAILS
Check on any practical matters such as remaining sessions, fees, or paperwork. Make sure you're clear about how any outstanding matters will be handled. If you're part of an ongoing treatment plan, confirm the best steps to transition out.

8. TAKE CARE OF YOURSELF
Ending therapy can stir up emotions, and that's normal. Be sure to practice self-care and seek additional support if needed during the transition. Whether it's reaching out to a trusted friend, journaling, or engaging in activities that help ground you, take the time to nurture yourself after this change.

MY SAFETY PLAN

BECAUSE YOUR WELL-BEING MATTERS—ESPECIALLY ON THE HARD DAYS.
Life can feel heavy sometimes. When you're overwhelmed, anxious, or emotionally flooded, it's easy to forget what helps or who to turn to. That's where the following page comes in.

Think of *My Safety Net* as your personal care plan—something you create now to support yourself later. It's a place to list your go-to coping tools, your support system, and the reminders that help you feel grounded when things feel out of control.

Whether it's someone to call, a space to breathe, or a gentle truth to hold onto, this plan is here to catch you when you need it most. You deserve to feel safe, supported, and never alone in your struggle.

WHAT IS A SAFETY PLAN?
A safety plan is a practical, personalized tool designed to help you navigate moments of emotional crisis, distress, or potential harm. It includes strategies and supports that help reduce risk, increase safety, and restore a sense of control. This can be particularly helpful for managing:
- Suicidal thoughts or urges
- Self-harm behaviors
- Panic attacks
- Episodes of dissociation
- Overwhelming stress or anxiety

YOUR SAFETY PLAN ACTS AS A PREVENTION TOOL: CREATED WHEN YOU ARE CALM AND CLEAR, SO IT'S AVAILABLE WHEN YOU MAY NOT BE.

MY SAFETY PLAN

MY WARNING SIGNS ARE...

3 PEOPLE THAT CALM ME

MY SAFE WORD IS...

2 PEOPLE THAT MAKE ME LAUGH

MY SAFE PLACE IS...

1 PERSON I CAN BE COMPLETELY HONEST WITH

MY COPING SKILLS ARE...

IN THE EVENT OF A CRISIS

CALL EMERGENCY CONTACT #1:
CALL CRISIS HOTLINE: 988
CALL EMERGENCY SERVICES: 911

THERAPIST INTERVIEW

Learn about your therapist and
determine if they are a good fit for you.

WHY DID YOU BECOME A THERAPIST?
_____
_____
_____
_____
_____

HOW LONG HAVE YOU BEEN PRACTICING THERAPY?
_____
_____
_____
_____
_____

DO YOU HAVE EXPERIENCE PROVIDING THERAPY TO PEOPLE WITH SIMILAR ISSUES AS MINE?
_____
_____
_____
_____
_____

WHAT ARE YOUR POLICIES AROUND CANCELLATIONS, INSURANCE, AND PAYMENTS?
_____
_____
_____
_____
_____

HOW SHOULD I PREPARE FOR MY FIRST SESSION?

_____
_____
_____
_____
_____
_____

HOW DO YOU APPROACH TREATMENT? WHAT CLINICAL MODALITIES DO YOU USE?

_____
_____
_____
_____
_____
_____

WILL YOU GIVE ME HOMEWORK IN BETWEEN SESSIONS?

_____
_____
_____
_____
_____
_____

THERAPIST INTERVIEW

Learn about your therapist and
determine if they are a good fit for you.

WHY DID YOU BECOME A THERAPIST?
_____
_____
_____
_____
_____

HOW LONG HAVE YOU BEEN PRACTICING THERAPY?
_____
_____
_____
_____
_____

DO YOU HAVE EXPERIENCE PROVIDING THERAPY TO PEOPLE WITH SIMILAR ISSUES AS MINE?
_____
_____
_____
_____
_____

WHAT ARE YOUR POLICIES AROUND CANCELLATIONS, INSURANCE, AND PAYMENTS?
_____
_____
_____
_____
_____

HOW SHOULD I PREPARE FOR MY FIRST SESSION?

_____
_____
_____
_____
_____
_____
_____

HOW DO YOU APPROACH TREATMENT? WHAT CLINICAL MODALITIES DO YOU USE?

_____
_____
_____
_____
_____
_____
_____

WILL YOU GIVE ME HOMEWORK IN BETWEEN SESSIONS?

_____
_____
_____
_____
_____
_____
_____

THERAPIST INTERVIEW

Learn about your therapist and
determine if they are a good fit for you.

WHY DID YOU BECOME A THERAPIST?
___
___
___
___
___

HOW LONG HAVE YOU BEEN PRACTICING THERAPY?
___
___
___
___
___

DO YOU HAVE EXPERIENCE PROVIDING THERAPY TO PEOPLE WITH SIMILAR ISSUES AS MINE?
___
___
___
___
___

WHAT ARE YOUR POLICIES AROUND CANCELLATIONS, INSURANCE, AND PAYMENTS?
___
___
___
___
___

HOW SHOULD I PREPARE FOR MY FIRST SESSION?
_____
_____
_____
_____
_____
_____

HOW DO YOU APPROACH TREATMENT? WHAT CLINICAL MODALITIES DO YOU USE?
_____
_____
_____
_____
_____
_____

WILL YOU GIVE ME HOMEWORK IN BETWEEN SESSIONS?
_____
_____
_____
_____
_____
_____

THERAPIST INTERVIEW

Learn about your therapist and
determine if they are a good fit for you.

WHY DID YOU BECOME A THERAPIST?
_____
_____
_____
_____
_____

HOW LONG HAVE YOU BEEN PRACTICING THERAPY?
_____
_____
_____
_____
_____

DO YOU HAVE EXPERIENCE PROVIDING THERAPY TO PEOPLE WITH SIMILAR ISSUES AS MINE?
_____
_____
_____
_____
_____

WHAT ARE YOUR POLICIES AROUND CANCELLATIONS, INSURANCE, AND PAYMENTS?
_____
_____
_____
_____
_____

HOW SHOULD I PREPARE FOR MY FIRST SESSION?
_____
_____
_____
_____
_____
_____
_____

HOW DO YOU APPROACH TREATMENT? WHAT CLINICAL MODALITIES DO YOU USE?
_____
_____
_____
_____
_____
_____
_____

WILL YOU GIVE ME HOMEWORK IN BETWEEN SESSIONS?
_____
_____
_____
_____
_____
_____
_____

THERAPIST INTERVIEW

Learn about your therapist and
determine if they are a good fit for you.

WHY DID YOU BECOME A THERAPIST?
_____
_____
_____
_____
_____

HOW LONG HAVE YOU BEEN PRACTICING THERAPY?
_____
_____
_____
_____
_____

DO YOU HAVE EXPERIENCE PROVIDING THERAPY TO PEOPLE WITH SIMILAR ISSUES AS MINE?
_____
_____
_____
_____
_____

WHAT ARE YOUR POLICIES AROUND CANCELLATIONS, INSURANCE, AND PAYMENTS?
_____
_____
_____
_____
_____

HOW SHOULD I PREPARE FOR MY FIRST SESSION?
_____
_____
_____
_____
_____
_____
_____

HOW DO YOU APPROACH TREATMENT? WHAT CLINICAL MODALITIES DO YOU USE?
_____
_____
_____
_____
_____
_____
_____

WILL YOU GIVE ME HOMEWORK IN BETWEEN SESSIONS?
_____
_____
_____
_____
_____
_____
_____

THERAPY APPOINTMENT TRACKER

DATE	TIME
DATE	TIME
DATE	TIME
DATE	TIME
DATE	TIME
DATE	TIME
DATE	TIME
DATE	TIME
DATE	TIME
DATE	TIME
DATE	TIME
DATE	TIME
DATE	TIME
DATE	TIME

THERAPY APPOINTMENT TRACKER

DATE	TIME
DATE	TIME
DATE	TIME
DATE	TIME
DATE	TIME
DATE	TIME
DATE	TIME
DATE	TIME
DATE	TIME
DATE	TIME
DATE	TIME
DATE	TIME
DATE	TIME
DATE	TIME

THERAPY APPOINTMENT TRACKER

DATE	TIME

THERAPY APPOINTMENT TRACKER

DATE	TIME

THERAPY APPOINTMENT TRACKER

DATE		TIME	
DATE		TIME	
DATE		TIME	
DATE		TIME	
DATE		TIME	
DATE		TIME	
DATE		TIME	
DATE		TIME	
DATE		TIME	
DATE		TIME	
DATE		TIME	
DATE		TIME	
DATE		TIME	
DATE		TIME	

THERAPY APPOINTMENT TRACKER

DATE	TIME
DATE	TIME
DATE	TIME
DATE	TIME
DATE	TIME
DATE	TIME
DATE	TIME
DATE	TIME
DATE	TIME
DATE	TIME
DATE	TIME
DATE	TIME
DATE	TIME
DATE	TIME

THERAPY APPOINTMENT TRACKER

DATE	TIME
DATE	TIME
DATE	TIME
DATE	TIME
DATE	TIME
DATE	TIME
DATE	TIME
DATE	TIME
DATE	TIME
DATE	TIME
DATE	TIME
DATE	TIME
DATE	TIME
DATE	TIME

THERAPY APPOINTMENT TRACKER

DATE	TIME

THERAPY APPOINTMENT TRACKER

DATE	TIME
DATE	TIME
DATE	TIME
DATE	TIME
DATE	TIME
DATE	TIME
DATE	TIME
DATE	TIME
DATE	TIME
DATE	TIME
DATE	TIME
DATE	TIME
DATE	TIME
DATE	TIME

THERAPY APPOINTMENT TRACKER

DATE	TIME
DATE	TIME
DATE	TIME
DATE	TIME
DATE	TIME
DATE	TIME
DATE	TIME
DATE	TIME
DATE	TIME
DATE	TIME
DATE	TIME
DATE	TIME
DATE	TIME
DATE	TIME

MENTAL HEALTH MEDICATION

Category	Conditions	Common Medications	Time Effect
ANTI-ANXIETY	anxiety disorders, panic attacks	valium, xanax	immediate to several weeks
ANTI-DEPRESSANTS	depression also used to treat some anxiety disorders	prozac, cymbalta	between 4-8 weeks
ANTI-PSYCHOTICS	schizophrenia bipolar disorder, severe depression	risperdal, zyprexa	days to several weeks
MOOD STABILIZERS	bipolar disorder	lithium, depakote	days to several weeks
STIMULANTS	adhd, narcolepsy	adderall, ritalin	immediate to several hours

MEDICATION SIDE EFFECTS

A SIDE EFFECT IS A SECONDARY, TYPICALLY UNDESIRABLE EFFECT OF A DRUG OR MEDICAL TREATMENT. IF YOU'RE EXPERIENCING ANY OF THE FOLLOWING SIDE EFFECTS, PLEASE CHECK BELOW:

- ☐ ANXIOUSNESS
- ☐ CONSTIPATION
- ☐ CRAMPS
- ☐ DEPRESSION
- ☐ DIZZINESS
- ☐ DRY MOUTH
- ☐ FATIGUE
- ☐ HEADACHES
- ☐ IRRITABILITY

- ☐ LOSS OF SEX DRIVE
- ☐ MEMORY LOSS
- ☐ MUSCLE SPAMS
- ☐ NAUSEA
- ☐ PARANOIA
- ☐ PERSONALITY CHANGES
- ☐ SLEEP PROBLEMS
- ☐ WEIGHT GAIN
- ☐ WEIGHT LOSS

OTHER SIDE EFFECTS YOU'VE EXPERIENCED:

WHILE SIDE EFFECTS ARE COMMON WHEN STARTING A NEW MEDICATION, PLEASE TALK TO YOUR DOCTOR ABOUT THEM.

MEDICATION TRACKER

MEDICATION	DOSE	FREQUENCY	TIME

ANY SIDE EFFECTS?

NOTES:

MEDICATION SIDE EFFECTS

A SIDE EFFECT IS A SECONDARY, TYPICALLY UNDESIRABLE EFFECT OF A DRUG OR MEDICAL TREATMENT. IF YOU'RE EXPERIENCING ANY OF THE FOLLOWING SIDE EFFECTS, PLEASE CHECK BELOW:

- ANXIOUSNESS
- CONSTIPATION
- CRAMPS
- DEPRESSION
- DIZZINESS
- DRY MOUTH
- FATIGUE
- HEADACHES
- IRRITABILITY

- LOSS OF SEX DRIVE
- MEMORY LOSS
- MUSCLE SPAMS
- NAUSEA
- PARANOIA
- PERSONALITY CHANGES
- SLEEP PROBLEMS
- WEIGHT GAIN
- WEIGHT LOSS

OTHER SIDE EFFECTS YOU'VE EXPERIENCED:

WHILE SIDE EFFECTS ARE COMMON WHEN STARTING A NEW MEDICATION, PLEASE TALK TO YOUR DOCTOR ABOUT THEM.

MEDICATION TRACKER

MEDICATION	DOSE	FREQUENCY	TIME

ANY SIDE EFFECTS?

NOTES:

MEDICATION SIDE EFFECTS

A SIDE EFFECT IS A SECONDARY, TYPICALLY UNDESIRABLE EFFECT OF A DRUG OR MEDICAL TREATMENT. IF YOU'RE EXPERIENCING ANY OF THE FOLLOWING SIDE EFFECTS, PLEASE CHECK BELOW:

- ANXIOUSNESS
- CONSTIPATION
- CRAMPS
- DEPRESSION
- DIZZINESS
- DRY MOUTH
- FATIGUE
- HEADACHES
- IRRITABILITY
- LOSS OF SEX DRIVE
- MEMORY LOSS
- MUSCLE SPAMS
- NAUSEA
- PARANOIA
- PERSONALITY CHANGES
- SLEEP PROBLEMS
- WEIGHT GAIN
- WEIGHT LOSS

OTHER SIDE EFFECTS YOU'VE EXPERIENCED:

WHILE SIDE EFFECTS ARE COMMON WHEN STARTING A NEW MEDICATION, PLEASE TALK TO YOUR DOCTOR ABOUT THEM.

MEDICATION TRACKER

MEDICATION	DOSE	FREQUENCY	TIME

ANY SIDE EFFECTS?

NOTES:

SAVE IT FOR THERAPY

Therapy Session Homework

SAVE IT FOR THERAPY

Affirmations for Self-Love

♡ I LOVE WHO I AM AND WHO I AM BECOMING.

♡ I AM WORTHY OF LOVE AND RESPECT.

♡ I AM ENOUGH!

♡ I CHOOSE JOY AND HAPPINESS.

♡ I VALUE MY BODY AND WHAT IT DOES FOR ME.

THERAPY SESSION RECAP

DATE __/__/____

THINGS I WANT TO TALK ABOUT TODAY:

_____
_____
_____
_____

SESSION NOTES:

HOMEWORK ASSIGNMENT:

THERAPY HOMEWORK ASSIGNMENT

GEMS MY THERAPIST DROPPED

USE THIS SPACE TO JOT DOWN ANY INSIGHTFUL OR MEANINGFUL STATEMENTS YOUR THERAPIST SHARED DURING YOUR SESSIONS.

_____
_____
_____
_____
_____
_____
_____
_____
_____
_____
_____
_____
_____
_____
_____
_____

THERAPY SESSION RECAP

DATE __/__/____

THINGS I WANT TO TALK ABOUT TODAY:

_____
_____
_____
_____

SESSION NOTES:

HOMEWORK ASSIGNMENT:

THERAPY HOMEWORK ASSIGNMENT

GEMS MY THERAPIST DROPPED

USE THIS SPACE TO JOT DOWN ANY INSIGHTFUL OR MEANINGFUL STATEMENTS YOUR THERAPIST SHARED DURING YOUR SESSIONS.

_____
_____
_____
_____
_____
_____
_____
_____
_____
_____
_____
_____
_____
_____
_____
_____
_____
_____

THERAPY SESSION RECAP

DATE __/__/____

THINGS I WANT TO TALK ABOUT TODAY:

_____
_____
_____
_____

SESSION NOTES:

HOMEWORK ASSIGNMENT:

THERAPY HOMEWORK ASSIGNMENT

GEMS MY THERAPIST DROPPED

USE THIS SPACE TO JOT DOWN ANY INSIGHTFUL OR MEANINGFUL STATEMENTS YOUR THERAPIST SHARED DURING YOUR SESSIONS.

THERAPY SESSION RECAP

DATE __/__/____

THINGS I WANT TO TALK ABOUT TODAY:

_____
_____
_____
_____

SESSION NOTES:

HOMEWORK ASSIGNMENT:

THERAPY HOMEWORK ASSIGNMENT

GEMS MY THERAPIST DROPPED

USE THIS SPACE TO JOT DOWN ANY INSIGHTFUL OR MEANINGFUL STATEMENTS YOUR THERAPIST SHARED DURING YOUR SESSIONS.

_____
_____
_____
_____
_____
_____
_____
_____
_____
_____
_____
_____
_____
_____
_____
_____
_____
_____

THERAPY SESSION RECAP

DATE __/__/____

THINGS I WANT TO TALK ABOUT TODAY:

_____
_____
_____
_____

SESSION NOTES:

HOMEWORK ASSIGNMENT:

THERAPY HOMEWORK ASSIGNMENT

GEMS MY THERAPIST DROPPED

USE THIS SPACE TO JOT DOWN ANY INSIGHTFUL OR MEANINGFUL STATEMENTS YOUR THERAPIST SHARED DURING YOUR SESSIONS.

_____
_____
_____
_____
_____
_____
_____
_____
_____
_____
_____
_____
_____

THERAPY SESSION RECAP

DATE __/__/____

THINGS I WANT TO TALK ABOUT TODAY:

_____
_____
_____
_____

SESSION NOTES:

HOMEWORK ASSIGNMENT:

THERAPY HOMEWORK ASSIGNMENT

GEMS MY THERAPIST DROPPED

USE THIS SPACE TO JOT DOWN ANY INSIGHTFUL OR MEANINGFUL STATEMENTS YOUR THERAPIST SHARED DURING YOUR SESSIONS.

_____
_____
_____
_____
_____
_____
_____
_____
_____
_____
_____
_____
_____
_____
_____
_____

THERAPY SESSION RECAP

DATE __/__/____

THINGS I WANT TO TALK ABOUT TODAY:

_____
_____
_____
_____

SESSION NOTES:

HOMEWORK ASSIGNMENT:

THERAPY HOMEWORK ASSIGNMENT

GEMS MY THERAPIST DROPPED

USE THIS SPACE TO JOT DOWN ANY INSIGHTFUL OR MEANINGFUL STATEMENTS YOUR THERAPIST SHARED DURING YOUR SESSIONS.

_____
_____
_____
_____
_____
_____
_____
_____
_____
_____
_____
_____
_____
_____
_____

THERAPY SESSION RECAP

DATE __/__/____

THINGS I WANT TO TALK ABOUT TODAY:

_____
_____
_____
_____

SESSION NOTES:

HOMEWORK ASSIGNMENT:

THERAPY HOMEWORK ASSIGNMENT

GEMS MY THERAPIST DROPPED

USE THIS SPACE TO JOT DOWN ANY INSIGHTFUL OR MEANINGFUL STATEMENTS YOUR THERAPIST SHARED DURING YOUR SESSIONS.

_____
_____
_____
_____
_____
_____
_____
_____
_____
_____
_____
_____
_____
_____
_____
_____

THERAPY SESSION RECAP

DATE __/__/____

THINGS I WANT TO TALK ABOUT TODAY:

_____
_____
_____
_____

SESSION NOTES:

HOMEWORK ASSIGNMENT:

THERAPY HOMEWORK ASSIGNMENT

GEMS MY THERAPIST DROPPED

USE THIS SPACE TO JOT DOWN ANY INSIGHTFUL OR MEANINGFUL STATEMENTS YOUR THERAPIST SHARED DURING YOUR SESSIONS.

_____
_____
_____
_____
_____
_____
_____
_____
_____
_____
_____
_____
_____
_____
_____
_____

THERAPY SESSION RECAP

DATE __/__/____

THINGS I WANT TO TALK ABOUT TODAY:

_____
_____
_____
_____

SESSION NOTES:

HOMEWORK ASSIGNMENT:

THERAPY HOMEWORK ASSIGNMENT

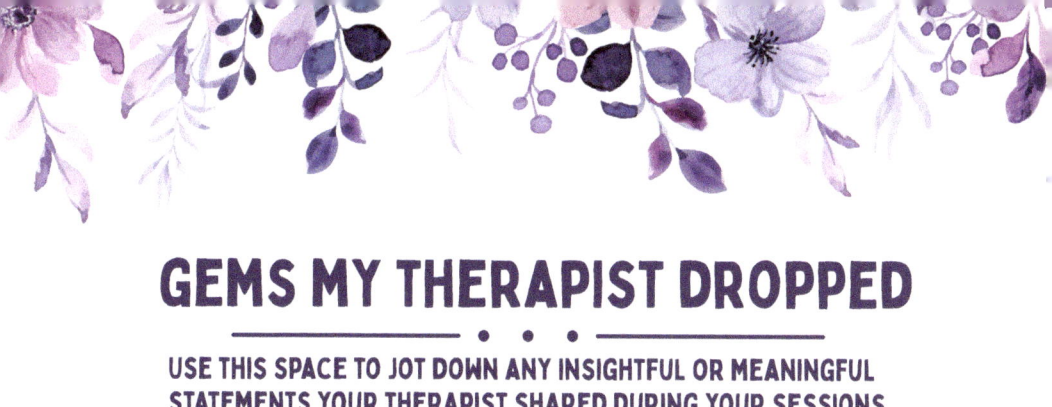

GEMS MY THERAPIST DROPPED

USE THIS SPACE TO JOT DOWN ANY INSIGHTFUL OR MEANINGFUL STATEMENTS YOUR THERAPIST SHARED DURING YOUR SESSIONS.

_____
_____
_____
_____
_____
_____
_____
_____
_____
_____
_____
_____
_____
_____
_____
_____

THERAPY SESSION RECAP

DATE __ / __ / ____

THINGS I WANT TO TALK ABOUT TODAY:

_____
_____
_____
_____

SESSION NOTES:

HOMEWORK ASSIGNMENT:

THERAPY HOMEWORK ASSIGNMENT

GEMS MY THERAPIST DROPPED

USE THIS SPACE TO JOT DOWN ANY INSIGHTFUL OR MEANINGFUL STATEMENTS YOUR THERAPIST SHARED DURING YOUR SESSIONS.

_____
_____
_____
_____
_____
_____
_____
_____
_____
_____
_____
_____
_____
_____
_____

THERAPY SESSION RECAP

DATE __/__/____

THINGS I WANT TO TALK ABOUT TODAY:

_____
_____
_____
_____

SESSION NOTES:

HOMEWORK ASSIGNMENT:

THERAPY HOMEWORK ASSIGNMENT

GEMS MY THERAPIST DROPPED

USE THIS SPACE TO JOT DOWN ANY INSIGHTFUL OR MEANINGFUL STATEMENTS YOUR THERAPIST SHARED DURING YOUR SESSIONS.

THERAPY SESSION RECAP

DATE __/__/____

THINGS I WANT TO TALK ABOUT TODAY:

_____
_____
_____
_____

SESSION NOTES:

HOMEWORK ASSIGNMENT:

THERAPY HOMEWORK ASSIGNMENT

GEMS MY THERAPIST DROPPED

USE THIS SPACE TO JOT DOWN ANY INSIGHTFUL OR MEANINGFUL STATEMENTS YOUR THERAPIST SHARED DURING YOUR SESSIONS.

_____
_____
_____
_____
_____
_____
_____
_____
_____
_____
_____
_____
_____
_____
_____
_____

THERAPY SESSION RECAP

DATE __/__/____

THINGS I WANT TO TALK ABOUT TODAY:

_____
_____
_____
_____

SESSION NOTES:

HOMEWORK ASSIGNMENT:

THERAPY HOMEWORK ASSIGNMENT

GEMS MY THERAPIST DROPPED

USE THIS SPACE TO JOT DOWN ANY INSIGHTFUL OR MEANINGFUL STATEMENTS YOUR THERAPIST SHARED DURING YOUR SESSIONS.

_____
_____
_____
_____
_____
_____
_____
_____
_____
_____
_____
_____
_____
_____
_____
_____

THERALY SESSION RECAP

DATE __/__/____

THINGS I WANT TO TALK ABOUT TODAY:

_____
_____
_____
_____

SESSION NOTES:

HOMEWORK ASSIGNMENT:

THERAPY HOMEWORK ASSIGNMENT

GEMS MY THERAPIST DROPPED

USE THIS SPACE TO JOT DOWN ANY INSIGHTFUL OR MEANINGFUL STATEMENTS YOUR THERAPIST SHARED DURING YOUR SESSIONS.

THERAPY SESSION RECAP

DATE __/__/____

THINGS I WANT TO TALK ABOUT TODAY:

_____
_____
_____
_____

SESSION NOTES:

HOMEWORK ASSIGNMENT:

THERAPY HOMEWORK ASSIGNMENT

GEMS MY THERAPIST DROPPED

USE THIS SPACE TO JOT DOWN ANY INSIGHTFUL OR MEANINGFUL STATEMENTS YOUR THERAPIST SHARED DURING YOUR SESSIONS.

_____
_____
_____
_____
_____
_____
_____
_____
_____
_____
_____
_____
_____
_____
_____
_____
_____

THERAPY SESSION RECAP

DATE __/__/____

THINGS I WANT TO TALK ABOUT TODAY:

_____
_____
_____
_____

SESSION NOTES:

HOMEWORK ASSIGNMENT:

THERAPY HOMEWORK ASSIGNMENT

GEMS MY THERAPIST DROPPED

USE THIS SPACE TO JOT DOWN ANY INSIGHTFUL OR MEANINGFUL STATEMENTS YOUR THERAPIST SHARED DURING YOUR SESSIONS.

_____
_____
_____
_____
_____
_____
_____
_____
_____
_____
_____
_____
_____
_____
_____
_____
_____
_____

THERAPY SESSION RECAP

DATE __/__/____

THINGS I WANT TO TALK ABOUT TODAY:

_____
_____
_____
_____

SESSION NOTES:

HOMEWORK ASSIGNMENT:

THERAPY HOMEWORK ASSIGNMENT

GEMS MY THERAPIST DROPPED

USE THIS SPACE TO JOT DOWN ANY INSIGHTFUL OR MEANINGFUL STATEMENTS YOUR THERAPIST SHARED DURING YOUR SESSIONS.

_____
_____
_____
_____
_____
_____
_____
_____
_____
_____
_____
_____
_____
_____

THERAPY SESSION RECAP

DATE __/__/____

THINGS I WANT TO TALK ABOUT TODAY:

_____
_____
_____
_____

SESSION NOTES:

HOMEWORK ASSIGNMENT:

THERAPY HOMEWORK ASSIGNMENT

GEMS MY THERAPIST DROPPED

USE THIS SPACE TO JOT DOWN ANY INSIGHTFUL OR MEANINGFUL STATEMENTS YOUR THERAPIST SHARED DURING YOUR SESSIONS.

_____
_____
_____
_____
_____
_____
_____
_____
_____
_____
_____
_____
_____
_____
_____
_____

THERAPY SESSION RECAP

DATE __/__/____

THINGS I WANT TO TALK ABOUT TODAY:

_____
_____
_____
_____

SESSION NOTES:

HOMEWORK ASSIGNMENT:

THERAPY HOMEWORK ASSIGNMENT

GEMS MY THERAPIST DROPPED

USE THIS SPACE TO JOT DOWN ANY INSIGHTFUL OR MEANINGFUL STATEMENTS YOUR THERAPIST SHARED DURING YOUR SESSIONS.

_____
_____
_____
_____
_____
_____
_____
_____
_____
_____
_____
_____
_____
_____
_____
_____
_____
_____

Save It For Therapy

Feelings Wheel
Trigger Tracker

SAVE IT FOR THERAPY

Affirmations for Anxiety

- I INHALE PEACE AND EXHALE WORRY.

- THIS FEELING IS ONLY TEMPORARY.

- I AM LOVED AND ACCEPTED JUST AS I AM.

- I RELEASE WORRY AND WELCOME PEACE.

- I AM SAFE AND PROTECTED.

BUT HOW ARE YOU REALLY FEELING?

WHEN CONSIDERING YOUR EMOTIONS, WHAT SPECIFIC WORDS COME TO MIND? USE THE EMOTION WHEEL BELOW WHEN YOU'RE HAVING TROUBLE NAMING THE FEELING.

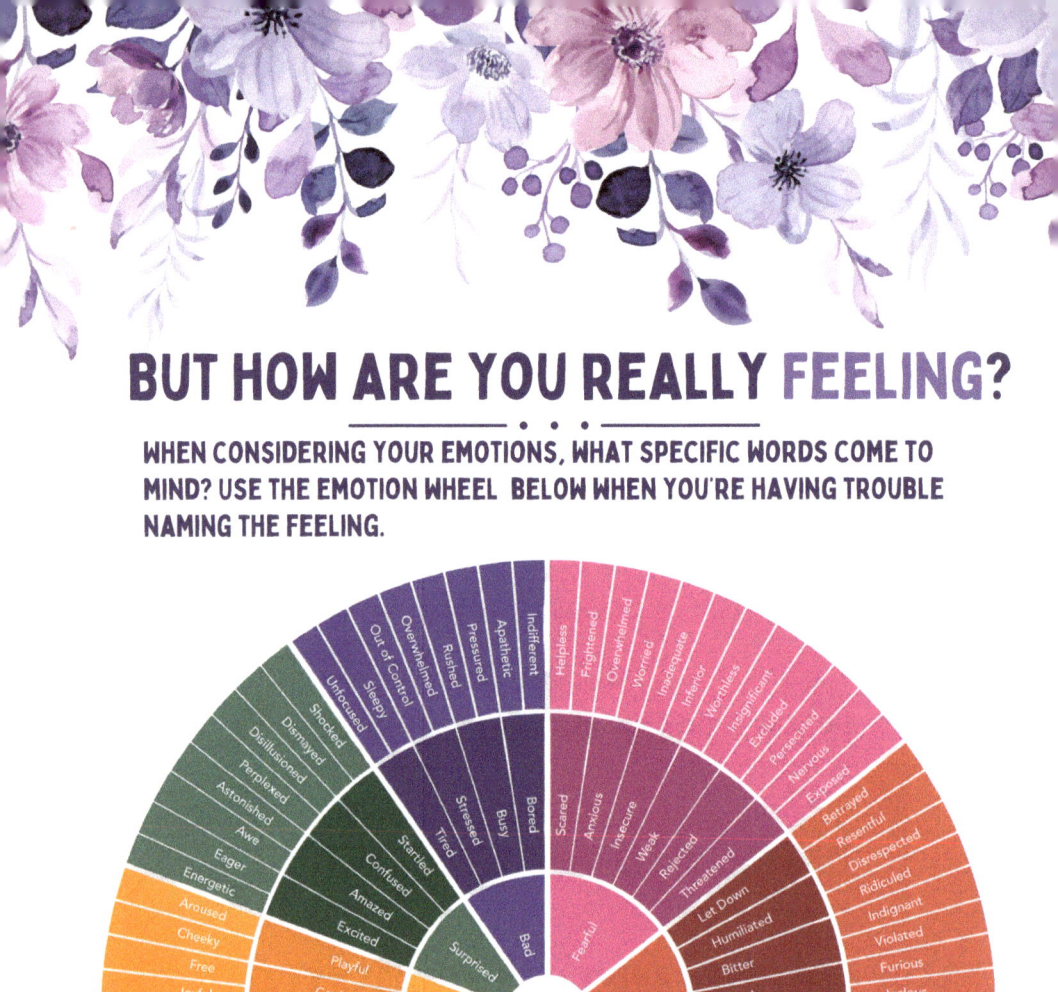

TRIGGER TRACKER

DATE:

WHAT HAPPENED?

TIME:

HOW DID IT MAKE YOU FEEL?

DATE:

WHAT HAPPENED?

TIME:

HOW DID IT MAKE YOU FEEL?

DATE:

WHAT HAPPENED?

TIME:

HOW DID IT MAKE YOU FEEL?

TRIGGER TRACKER

DATE:

TIME:

WHAT HAPPENED?

HOW DID IT MAKE YOU FEEL?

DATE:

TIME:

WHAT HAPPENED?

HOW DID IT MAKE YOU FEEL?

DATE:

TIME:

WHAT HAPPENED?

HOW DID IT MAKE YOU FEEL?

TRIGGER TRACKER

DATE:

TIME:

WHAT HAPPENED?

HOW DID IT MAKE YOU FEEL?

DATE:

TIME:

WHAT HAPPENED?

HOW DID IT MAKE YOU FEEL?

DATE:

TIME:

WHAT HAPPENED?

HOW DID IT MAKE YOU FEEL?

TRIGGER TRACKER

DATE:

TIME:

WHAT HAPPENED?

HOW DID IT MAKE YOU FEEL?

DATE:

TIME:

WHAT HAPPENED?

HOW DID IT MAKE YOU FEEL?

DATE:

TIME:

WHAT HAPPENED?

HOW DID IT MAKE YOU FEEL?

TRIGGER TRACKER

DATE: **TIME:**

WHAT HAPPENED?

HOW DID IT MAKE YOU FEEL?

DATE: **TIME:**

WHAT HAPPENED?

HOW DID IT MAKE YOU FEEL?

DATE: **TIME:**

WHAT HAPPENED?

HOW DID IT MAKE YOU FEEL?

TRIGGER TRACKER

DATE:

TIME:

WHAT HAPPENED?

HOW DID IT MAKE YOU FEEL?

DATE:

TIME:

WHAT HAPPENED?

HOW DID IT MAKE YOU FEEL?

DATE:

TIME:

WHAT HAPPENED?

HOW DID IT MAKE YOU FEEL?

TRIGGER TRACKER

DATE:

TIME:

WHAT HAPPENED?

HOW DID IT MAKE YOU FEEL?

DATE:

TIME:

WHAT HAPPENED?

HOW DID IT MAKE YOU FEEL?

DATE:

TIME:

WHAT HAPPENED?

HOW DID IT MAKE YOU FEEL?

TRIGGER TRACKER

DATE: **TIME:**

WHAT HAPPENED? **HOW DID IT MAKE YOU FEEL?**

DATE: **TIME:**

WHAT HAPPENED? **HOW DID IT MAKE YOU FEEL?**

DATE: **TIME:**

WHAT HAPPENED? **HOW DID IT MAKE YOU FEEL?**

TRIGGER TRACKER

DATE:

WHAT HAPPENED?

TIME:

HOW DID IT MAKE YOU FEEL?

DATE:

WHAT HAPPENED?

TIME:

HOW DID IT MAKE YOU FEEL?

DATE:

WHAT HAPPENED?

TIME:

HOW DID IT MAKE YOU FEEL?

TRIGGER TRACKER

DATE:

WHAT HAPPENED?

TIME:

HOW DID IT MAKE YOU FEEL?

DATE:

WHAT HAPPENED?

TIME:

HOW DID IT MAKE YOU FEEL?

DATE:

WHAT HAPPENED?

TIME:

HOW DID IT MAKE YOU FEEL?

TRIGGER TRACKER

DATE:

WHAT HAPPENED?

TIME:

HOW DID IT MAKE YOU FEEL?

DATE:

WHAT HAPPENED?

TIME:

HOW DID IT MAKE YOU FEEL?

DATE:

WHAT HAPPENED?

TIME:

HOW DID IT MAKE YOU FEEL?

TRIGGER TRACKER

DATE:

WHAT HAPPENED?

TIME:

HOW DID IT MAKE YOU FEEL?

DATE:

WHAT HAPPENED?

TIME:

HOW DID IT MAKE YOU FEEL?

DATE:

WHAT HAPPENED?

TIME:

HOW DID IT MAKE YOU FEEL?

TRIGGER TRACKER

DATE:

TIME:

WHAT HAPPENED?

HOW DID IT MAKE YOU FEEL?

DATE:

TIME:

WHAT HAPPENED?

HOW DID IT MAKE YOU FEEL?

DATE:

TIME:

WHAT HAPPENED?

HOW DID IT MAKE YOU FEEL?

TRIGGER TRACKER

DATE:

WHAT HAPPENED?

TIME:

HOW DID IT MAKE YOU FEEL?

DATE:

WHAT HAPPENED?

TIME:

HOW DID IT MAKE YOU FEEL?

DATE:

WHAT HAPPENED?

TIME:

HOW DID IT MAKE YOU FEEL?

TRIGGER TRACKER

DATE: **TIME:**

WHAT HAPPENED? **HOW DID IT MAKE YOU FEEL?**

DATE: **TIME:**

WHAT HAPPENED? **HOW DID IT MAKE YOU FEEL?**

DATE: **TIME:**

WHAT HAPPENED? **HOW DID IT MAKE YOU FEEL?**

TRIGGER TRACKER

DATE:

TIME:

WHAT HAPPENED?

HOW DID IT MAKE YOU FEEL?

DATE:

TIME:

WHAT HAPPENED?

HOW DID IT MAKE YOU FEEL?

DATE:

TIME:

WHAT HAPPENED?

HOW DID IT MAKE YOU FEEL?

TRIGGER TRACKER

DATE:

TIME:

WHAT HAPPENED?

HOW DID IT MAKE YOU FEEL?

DATE:

TIME:

WHAT HAPPENED?

HOW DID IT MAKE YOU FEEL?

DATE:

TIME:

WHAT HAPPENED?

HOW DID IT MAKE YOU FEEL?

TRIGGER TRACKER

DATE:

WHAT HAPPENED?

TIME:

HOW DID IT MAKE YOU FEEL?

DATE:

WHAT HAPPENED?

TIME:

HOW DID IT MAKE YOU FEEL?

DATE:

WHAT HAPPENED?

TIME:

HOW DID IT MAKE YOU FEEL?

TRIGGER TRACKER

DATE:

WHAT HAPPENED?

TIME:

HOW DID IT MAKE YOU FEEL?

DATE:

WHAT HAPPENED?

TIME:

HOW DID IT MAKE YOU FEEL?

DATE:

WHAT HAPPENED?

TIME:

HOW DID IT MAKE YOU FEEL?

TRIGGER TRACKER

DATE:

TIME:

WHAT HAPPENED?

HOW DID IT MAKE YOU FEEL?

DATE:

TIME:

WHAT HAPPENED?

HOW DID IT MAKE YOU FEEL?

DATE:

TIME:

WHAT HAPPENED?

HOW DID IT MAKE YOU FEEL?

SAVE IT FOR THERAPY

Daily Check-In Report
Brain Dump

SAVE IT FOR THERAPY

Affirmations for Depression

- ♡ MY DEPRESSION DOES NOT DEFINE ME.

- ♡ I AM VALUABLE EVEN WHEN I'M NOT PRODUCTIVE.

- ♡ IT IS OKAY TO FEEL SAD IN THIS MOMENT.

- ♡ I AM NAVIGATING MY DEPRESSION AS BEST AS I CAN.

- ♡ I AM STRONG AND RESILIENT.

DAILY CHECK-IN REPORT

DATE: _____

MO TU WE TH FR SA SU

HOW AM I FEELING THIS MORNING?
😈 GREAT ☺ GOOD 😐 OKAY
☹ NOT GOOD 🤢 AWFUL

MY SLEEP LAST NIGHT WAS
😈 ☺ 😐 ☹ 🤢

APPROX. HOURS _____

GET UP TIME: _____

TODAY I INTEND TO: _____
_____
_____
_____

WATER INTAKE (OUNCES)
8 16 24 32
40 48 56 64

HOW AM I FEELING THIS EVENING?
😈 ☺ 😐 ☹ 🤢

WHAT I ATE TODAY:

THREE THINGS THAT I AM GRATEFUL FOR:
_____
_____
_____

SELF CARE ACTIVITY OF THE DAY
_____
_____
_____

WHAT I MANAGED TO ACCOMPLISH TODAY || GO YOU!
_____
_____
_____

SOMETHING THAT MADE ME FEEL GOOD TODAY:

REFLECTIONS

BRAIN DUMP

A BRAIN DUMP IS A FREE-WRITING SESSION WHERE YOU UNLOAD ANYTHING ON YOUR MIND. USE THE SPACE BELOW TO WRITE OR DOODLE WHATEVER IS ON YOUR MIND IN THIS MOMENT. THE GOAL IS TO CLEAR SPACE IN YOUR BRAIN.

DAILY CHECK-IN REPORT

DATE: _____

MO TU WE TH FR SA SU

HOW AM I FEELING THIS MORNING?
- GREAT
- GOOD
- OKAY
- NOT GOOD
- AWFUL

MY SLEEP LAST NIGHT WAS

APPROX. HOURS _____

GET UP TIME: _____

TODAY I INTEND TO:
_____
_____
_____
_____

WATER INTAKE (OUNCES)
8 16 24 32
40 48 56 64

HOW AM I FEELING THIS EVENING?

WHAT I ATE TODAY:

THREE THINGS THAT I AM GRATEFUL FOR:
_____
_____
_____

SELF CARE ACTIVITY OF THE DAY
_____
_____
_____

WHAT I MANAGED TO ACCOMPLISH TODAY || GO YOU!
_____
_____
_____

SOMETHING THAT MADE ME FEEL GOOD TODAY:

REFLECTIONS

BRAIN DUMP

A BRAIN DUMP IS A FREE-WRITING SESSION WHERE YOU UNLOAD ANYTHING ON YOUR MIND. USE THE SPACE BELOW TO WRITE OR DOODLE WHATEVER IS ON YOUR MIND IN THIS MOMENT. THE GOAL IS TO CLEAR SPACE IN YOUR BRAIN.

DAILY CHECK-IN REPORT

DATE: _____

MO TU WE TH FR SA SU

HOW AM I FEELING THIS MORNING?
- GREAT
- GOOD
- OKAY
- NOT GOOD
- AWFUL

MY SLEEP LAST NIGHT WAS

APPROX. HOURS _____

GET UP TIME: _____

TODAY I INTEND TO: _____
_____
_____
_____

WATER INTAKE (OUNCES)

8 16 24 32
40 48 56 64

HOW AM I FEELING THIS EVENING?

WHAT I ATE TODAY:

THREE THINGS THAT I AM GRATEFUL FOR:
_____
_____
_____

SELF CARE ACTIVITY OF THE DAY
_____
_____
_____

WHAT I MANAGED TO ACCOMPLISH TODAY || GO YOU!
_____
_____
_____

SOMETHING THAT MADE ME FEEL GOOD TODAY:

REFLECTIONS

BRAIN DUMP

A BRAIN DUMP IS A FREE-WRITING SESSION WHERE YOU UNLOAD ANYTHING ON YOUR MIND. USE THE SPACE BELOW TO WRITE OR DOODLE WHATEVER IS ON YOUR MIND IN THIS MOMENT. THE GOAL IS TO CLEAR SPACE IN YOUR BRAIN.

DAILY CHECK-IN REPORT

DATE: _____

MO TU WE TH FR SA SU

HOW AM I FEELING THIS MORNING?
😊 GREAT 🙂 GOOD 😐 OKAY
😟 NOT GOOD 🤢 AWFUL

MY SLEEP LAST NIGHT WAS
😊 🙂 😐 😟 🤢

APPROX. HOURS _____

GET UP TIME: _____

TODAY I INTEND TO: _____
_____
_____
_____

WATER INTAKE (OUNCES)
8 16 24 32
40 48 56 64

HOW AM I FEELING THIS EVENING?
😊 🙂 😐 😟 🤢

WHAT I ATE TODAY:

THREE THINGS THAT I AM GRATEFUL FOR:
_____
_____
_____

SELF CARE ACTIVITY OF THE DAY
_____
_____
_____

WHAT I MANAGED TO ACCOMPLISH TODAY || GO YOU!
_____
_____
_____

SOMETHING THAT MADE ME FEEL GOOD TODAY:

REFLECTIONS

BRAIN DUMP

A BRAIN DUMP IS A FREE-WRITING SESSION WHERE YOU UNLOAD ANYTHING ON YOUR MIND. USE THE SPACE BELOW TO WRITE OR DOODLE WHATEVER IS ON YOUR MIND IN THIS MOMENT. THE GOAL IS TO CLEAR SPACE IN YOUR BRAIN.

DAILY CHECK-IN REPORT

DATE: _____

MO TU WE TH FR SA SU

HOW AM I FEELING THIS MORNING?
- 💜 GREAT
- 🙂 GOOD
- 😐 OKAY
- 😣 NOT GOOD
- 🤢 AWFUL

MY SLEEP LAST NIGHT WAS
💜 🙂 😐 😣 🤢

APPROX. HOURS _____

GET UP TIME: _____

TODAY I INTEND TO: _____
_____
_____
_____

WATER INTAKE (OUNCES)
8 16 24 32
40 48 56 64

HOW AM I FEELING THIS EVENING?
💜 🙂 😐 😣 🤢

WHAT I ATE TODAY:

THREE THINGS THAT I AM GRATEFUL FOR:
_____
_____
_____

SELF CARE ACTIVITY OF THE DAY
_____
_____
_____

WHAT I MANAGED TO ACCOMPLISH TODAY || GO YOU!
_____
_____
_____

SOMETHING THAT MADE ME FEEL GOOD TODAY:

REFLECTIONS

BRAIN DUMP

A BRAIN DUMP IS A FREE-WRITING SESSION WHERE YOU UNLOAD ANYTHING ON YOUR MIND. USE THE SPACE BELOW TO WRITE OR DOODLE WHATEVER IS ON YOUR MIND IN THIS MOMENT. THE GOAL IS TO CLEAR SPACE IN YOUR BRAIN.

DAILY CHECK-IN REPORT

DATE: _____

MO TU WE TH FR SA SU

HOW AM I FEELING THIS MORNING?
- 😍 GREAT
- 🙂 GOOD
- 😐 OKAY
- 😟 NOT GOOD
- 🤢 AWFUL

MY SLEEP LAST NIGHT WAS
😍 🙂 😐 😟 🤢

APPROX. HOURS _____

GET UP TIME: _____

TODAY I INTEND TO:
_____
_____
_____
_____

WATER INTAKE (OUNCES)
8 16 24 32
40 48 56 64

HOW AM I FEELING THIS EVENING?
😍 🙂 😐 😟 🤢

WHAT I ATE TODAY:

THREE THINGS THAT I AM GRATEFUL FOR:
_____
_____
_____

SELF CARE ACTIVITY OF THE DAY
_____
_____
_____

WHAT I MANAGED TO ACCOMPLISH TODAY || GO YOU!
_____
_____
_____

SOMETHING THAT MADE ME FEEL GOOD TODAY:

REFLECTIONS

BRAIN DUMP

A BRAIN DUMP IS A FREE-WRITING SESSION WHERE YOU UNLOAD ANYTHING ON YOUR MIND. USE THE SPACE BELOW TO WRITE OR DOODLE WHATEVER IS ON YOUR MIND IN THIS MOMENT. THE GOAL IS TO CLEAR SPACE IN YOUR BRAIN.

DAILY CHECK-IN REPORT

DATE: _____

MO TU WE TH FR SA SU

HOW AM I FEELING THIS MORNING?
😎 GREAT 🙂 GOOD 😐 OKAY
😣 NOT GOOD 🤢 AWFUL

MY SLEEP LAST NIGHT WAS
😎 🙂 😐 😣 🤢

APPROX. HOURS _____

GET UP TIME: _____

TODAY I INTEND TO: _____
_____
_____
_____

WATER INTAKE (OUNCES)
8 16 24 32
40 48 56 64

HOW AM I FEELING THIS EVENING?
😎 🙂 😐 😣 🤢

WHAT I ATE TODAY:

THREE THINGS THAT I AM GRATEFUL FOR:
_____
_____
_____

SELF CARE ACTIVITY OF THE DAY
_____
_____
_____

WHAT I MANAGED TO ACCOMPLISH TODAY || GO YOU!
_____
_____
_____

SOMETHING THAT MADE ME FEEL GOOD TODAY:

REFLECTIONS

BRAIN DUMP

A BRAIN DUMP IS A FREE-WRITING SESSION WHERE YOU UNLOAD ANYTHING ON YOUR MIND. USE THE SPACE BELOW TO WRITE OR DOODLE WHATEVER IS ON YOUR MIND IN THIS MOMENT. THE GOAL IS TO CLEAR SPACE IN YOUR BRAIN.

DAILY CHECK-IN REPORT

DATE: _____

(MO) (TU) (WE) (TH) (FR) (SA) (SU)

HOW AM I FEELING THIS MORNING?
- 😍 GREAT
- 🙂 GOOD
- 😐 OKAY
- ☹️ NOT GOOD
- 😖 AWFUL

MY SLEEP LAST NIGHT WAS
😍 🙂 😐 ☹️ 😖

APPROX. HOURS _____

GET UP TIME: _____

TODAY I INTEND TO:
_____
_____
_____
_____

WATER INTAKE (OUNCES)
(8) (16) (24) (32)
(40) (48) (56) (64)

HOW AM I FEELING THIS EVENING?
😍 🙂 😐 ☹️ 😖

WHAT I ATE TODAY:

THREE THINGS THAT I AM GRATEFUL FOR:
_____
_____
_____

SELF CARE ACTIVITY OF THE DAY
_____
_____
_____

WHAT I MANAGED TO ACCOMPLISH TODAY || GO YOU!
_____
_____
_____

SOMETHING THAT MADE ME FEEL GOOD TODAY:

REFLECTIONS

BRAIN DUMP

A BRAIN DUMP IS A FREE-WRITING SESSION WHERE YOU UNLOAD ANYTHING ON YOUR MIND. USE THE SPACE BELOW TO WRITE OR DOODLE WHATEVER IS ON YOUR MIND IN THIS MOMENT. THE GOAL IS TO CLEAR SPACE IN YOUR BRAIN.

DAILY CHECK-IN REPORT

DATE: _____

MO TU WE TH FR SA SU

HOW AM I FEELING THIS MORNING?
- 😍 GREAT
- 🙂 GOOD
- 😐 OKAY
- ☹️ NOT GOOD
- 😣 AWFUL

MY SLEEP LAST NIGHT WAS
😍 🙂 😐 ☹️ 😣

APPROX. HOURS _____

GET UP TIME: _____

TODAY I INTEND TO: _____
_____
_____
_____

WATER INTAKE (OUNCES)
8 16 24 32
40 48 56 64

HOW AM I FEELING THIS EVENING?
😍 🙂 😐 ☹️ 😣

WHAT I ATE TODAY:

THREE THINGS THAT I AM GRATEFUL FOR:
_____
_____
_____

SELF CARE ACTIVITY OF THE DAY
_____
_____
_____

WHAT I MANAGED TO ACCOMPLISH TODAY || GO YOU!
_____
_____
_____

SOMETHING THAT MADE ME FEEL GOOD TODAY:

REFLECTIONS

BRAIN DUMP

A BRAIN DUMP IS A FREE-WRITING SESSION WHERE YOU UNLOAD ANYTHING ON YOUR MIND. USE THE SPACE BELOW TO WRITE OR DOODLE WHATEVER IS ON YOUR MIND IN THIS MOMENT. THE GOAL IS TO CLEAR SPACE IN YOUR BRAIN.

DAILY CHECK-IN REPORT

DATE: _____

○ MO ○ TU ○ WE ○ TH ○ FR ○ SA ○ SU

HOW AM I FEELING THIS MORNING?
😎 GREAT ☺ GOOD 😐 OKAY
☹ NOT GOOD 😖 AWFUL

MY SLEEP LAST NIGHT WAS
😎 ☺ 😐 ☹ 😖

APPROX. HOURS _____

GET UP TIME: _____

TODAY I INTEND TO: _____
_____
_____
_____

WATER INTAKE (OUNCES)
○ 8 ○ 16 ○ 24 ○ 32
○ 40 ○ 48 ○ 56 ○ 64

HOW AM I FEELING THIS EVENING?
😎 ☺ 😐 ☹ 😖

WHAT I ATE TODAY:

THREE THINGS THAT I AM GRATEFUL FOR:
_____
_____
_____

SELF CARE ACTIVITY OF THE DAY
_____
_____
_____

WHAT I MANAGED TO ACCOMPLISH TODAY || GO YOU!
_____
_____
_____

SOMETHING THAT MADE ME FEEL GOOD TODAY:

REFLECTIONS

BRAIN DUMP

A BRAIN DUMP IS A FREE-WRITING SESSION WHERE YOU UNLOAD ANYTHING ON YOUR MIND. USE THE SPACE BELOW TO WRITE OR DOODLE WHATEVER IS ON YOUR MIND IN THIS MOMENT. THE GOAL IS TO CLEAR SPACE IN YOUR BRAIN.

DAILY CHECK-IN REPORT

DATE: _____

MO TU WE TH FR SA SU

HOW AM I FEELING THIS MORNING?

- 😎 GREAT
- 🙂 GOOD
- 😐 OKAY
- ☹️ NOT GOOD
- 😢 AWFUL

MY SLEEP LAST NIGHT WAS

😎 🙂 😐 ☹️ 😢

APPROX. HOURS _____

GET UP TIME: _____

TODAY I INTEND TO:
_____
_____
_____
_____

WATER INTAKE (OUNCES)

8 16 24 32
40 48 56 64

HOW AM I FEELING THIS EVENING?

😎 🙂 😐 ☹️ 😢

WHAT I ATE TODAY:

THREE THINGS THAT I AM GRATEFUL FOR:
_____
_____
_____

SELF CARE ACTIVITY OF THE DAY
_____
_____
_____

WHAT I MANAGED TO ACCOMPLISH TODAY || GO YOU!
_____
_____
_____

SOMETHING THAT MADE ME FEEL GOOD TODAY:

REFLECTIONS

BRAIN DUMP

A BRAIN DUMP IS A FREE-WRITING SESSION WHERE YOU UNLOAD ANYTHING ON YOUR MIND. USE THE SPACE BELOW TO WRITE OR DOODLE WHATEVER IS ON YOUR MIND IN THIS MOMENT. THE GOAL IS TO CLEAR SPACE IN YOUR BRAIN.

DAILY CHECK-IN REPORT

DATE: _____

MO TU WE TH FR SA SU

HOW AM I FEELING THIS MORNING?
- 😍 GREAT ☺ GOOD 😐 OKAY
- ☹ NOT GOOD 😢 AWFUL

MY SLEEP LAST NIGHT WAS
😍 ☺ 😐 ☹ 😢

APPROX. HOURS _____

GET UP TIME: _____

TODAY I INTEND TO:
_____
_____
_____
_____

WATER INTAKE (OUNCES)
8 16 24 32
40 48 56 64

HOW AM I FEELING THIS EVENING?
😍 ☺ 😐 ☹ 😢

WHAT I ATE TODAY:

THREE THINGS THAT I AM GRATEFUL FOR:
_____
_____
_____

SELF CARE ACTIVITY OF THE DAY
_____
_____

WHAT I MANAGED TO ACCOMPLISH TODAY || GO YOU!
_____
_____
_____

SOMETHING THAT MADE ME FEEL GOOD TODAY:

REFLECTIONS

BRAIN DUMP

A BRAIN DUMP IS A FREE-WRITING SESSION WHERE YOU UNLOAD ANYTHING ON YOUR MIND. USE THE SPACE BELOW TO WRITE OR DOODLE WHATEVER IS ON YOUR MIND IN THIS MOMENT. THE GOAL IS TO CLEAR SPACE IN YOUR BRAIN.

DAILY CHECK-IN REPORT

DATE: _____

MO TU WE TH FR SA SU

HOW AM I FEELING THIS MORNING?
- 😊 GREAT
- 🙂 GOOD
- 😐 OKAY
- ☹️ NOT GOOD
- 😢 AWFUL

MY SLEEP LAST NIGHT WAS
😊 🙂 😐 ☹️ 😢

APPROX. HOURS _____

GET UP TIME: _____

TODAY I INTEND TO:
_____
_____
_____

WATER INTAKE (OUNCES)
8 16 24 32
40 48 56 64

HOW AM I FEELING THIS EVENING?
😊 🙂 😐 ☹️ 😢

WHAT I ATE TODAY:

THREE THINGS THAT I AM GRATEFUL FOR:
_____
_____
_____

SELF CARE ACTIVITY OF THE DAY
_____
_____
_____

WHAT I MANAGED TO ACCOMPLISH TODAY || GO YOU!
_____
_____
_____

SOMETHING THAT MADE ME FEEL GOOD TODAY:

REFLECTIONS

BRAIN DUMP

A BRAIN DUMP IS A FREE-WRITING SESSION WHERE YOU UNLOAD ANYTHING ON YOUR MIND. USE THE SPACE BELOW TO WRITE OR DOODLE WHATEVER IS ON YOUR MIND IN THIS MOMENT. THE GOAL IS TO CLEAR SPACE IN YOUR BRAIN.

DAILY CHECK-IN REPORT

DATE: _____

(MO) (TU) (WE) (TH) (FR) (SA) (SU)

HOW AM I FEELING THIS MORNING?
- 😍 GREAT
- 🙂 GOOD
- 😐 OKAY
- ☹️ NOT GOOD
- 🤢 AWFUL

MY SLEEP LAST NIGHT WAS
😍 🙂 😐 ☹️ 🤢

APPROX. HOURS _____

GET UP TIME: _____

TODAY I INTEND TO: _____
_____
_____
_____

WATER INTAKE (OUNCES)
(8) (16) (24) (32)
(40) (48) (56) (64)

HOW AM I FEELING THIS EVENING?
😍 🙂 😐 ☹️ 🤢

WHAT I ATE TODAY:

THREE THINGS THAT I AM GRATEFUL FOR:
_____
_____
_____

SELF CARE ACTIVITY OF THE DAY
_____
_____
_____

WHAT I MANAGED TO ACCOMPLISH TODAY || GO YOU!
_____
_____
_____

SOMETHING THAT MADE ME FEEL GOOD TODAY:

REFLECTIONS

BRAIN DUMP

A BRAIN DUMP IS A FREE-WRITING SESSION WHERE YOU UNLOAD ANYTHING ON YOUR MIND. USE THE SPACE BELOW TO WRITE OR DOODLE WHATEVER IS ON YOUR MIND IN THIS MOMENT. THE GOAL IS TO CLEAR SPACE IN YOUR BRAIN.

DAILY CHECK-IN REPORT

DATE: _____

MO TU WE TH FR SA SU

HOW AM I FEELING THIS MORNING?
- GREAT
- GOOD
- OKAY
- NOT GOOD
- AWFUL

MY SLEEP LAST NIGHT WAS

APPROX. HOURS _____

GET UP TIME: _____

TODAY I INTEND TO:
_____
_____
_____
_____

WATER INTAKE (OUNCES)

8 16 24 32
40 48 56 64

HOW AM I FEELING THIS EVENING?

WHAT I ATE TODAY:

THREE THINGS THAT I AM GRATEFUL FOR:
_____
_____
_____

SELF CARE ACTIVITY OF THE DAY
_____
_____
_____

WHAT I MANAGED TO ACCOMPLISH TODAY || GO YOU!
_____
_____
_____

SOMETHING THAT MADE ME FEEL GOOD TODAY:

REFLECTIONS

BRAIN DUMP

——— • • • ———

A BRAIN DUMP IS A FREE-WRITING SESSION WHERE YOU UNLOAD ANYTHING ON YOUR MIND. USE THE SPACE BELOW TO WRITE OR DOODLE WHATEVER IS ON YOUR MIND IN THIS MOMENT. THE GOAL IS TO CLEAR SPACE IN YOUR BRAIN.

DAILY CHECK-IN REPORT

DATE: _____

MO TU WE TH FR SA SU

HOW AM I FEELING THIS MORNING?
😎 GREAT   🙂 GOOD   😐 OKAY
☹️ NOT GOOD   🤢 AWFUL

MY SLEEP LAST NIGHT WAS
😎 🙂 😐 ☹️ 🤢

APPROX. HOURS _____

GET UP TIME: _____

TODAY I INTEND TO: _____
_____
_____
_____

WATER INTAKE (OUNCES)
8 16 24 32
40 48 56 64

HOW AM I FEELING THIS EVENING?
😎 🙂 😐 ☹️ 🤢

WHAT I ATE TODAY:

THREE THINGS THAT I AM GRATEFUL FOR:
_____
_____
_____

SELF CARE ACTIVITY OF THE DAY
_____
_____
_____

WHAT I MANAGED TO ACCOMPLISH TODAY || GO YOU!
_____
_____
_____

SOMETHING THAT MADE ME FEEL GOOD TODAY:

REFLECTIONS

BRAIN DUMP

A BRAIN DUMP IS A FREE-WRITING SESSION WHERE YOU UNLOAD ANYTHING ON YOUR MIND. USE THE SPACE BELOW TO WRITE OR DOODLE WHATEVER IS ON YOUR MIND IN THIS MOMENT. THE GOAL IS TO CLEAR SPACE IN YOUR BRAIN.

DAILY CHECK-IN REPORT

DATE: _____

MO TU WE TH FR SA SU

HOW AM I FEELING THIS MORNING?
- 😎 GREAT
- 🙂 GOOD
- 😐 OKAY
- 🙁 NOT GOOD
- 🤢 AWFUL

MY SLEEP LAST NIGHT WAS
😎 🙂 😐 🙁 🤢

APPROX. HOURS _____

GET UP TIME: _____

TODAY I INTEND TO:
_____
_____
_____
_____

WATER INTAKE (OUNCES)
8 16 24 32
40 48 56 64

HOW AM I FEELING THIS EVENING?
😎 🙂 😐 🙁 🤢

WHAT I ATE TODAY:

THREE THINGS THAT I AM GRATEFUL FOR:
_____
_____
_____

SELF CARE ACTIVITY OF THE DAY
_____
_____
_____

WHAT I MANAGED TO ACCOMPLISH TODAY || GO YOU!
_____
_____
_____

SOMETHING THAT MADE ME FEEL GOOD TODAY:

REFLECTIONS

BRAIN DUMP

A BRAIN DUMP IS A FREE-WRITING SESSION WHERE YOU UNLOAD ANYTHING ON YOUR MIND. USE THE SPACE BELOW TO WRITE OR DOODLE WHATEVER IS ON YOUR MIND IN THIS MOMENT. THE GOAL IS TO CLEAR SPACE IN YOUR BRAIN.

DAILY CHECK-IN REPORT

DATE: _____

MO TU WE TH FR SA SU

HOW AM I FEELING THIS MORNING?
- 😍 GREAT
- 🙂 GOOD
- 😐 OKAY
- ☹️ NOT GOOD
- 😢 AWFUL

MY SLEEP LAST NIGHT WAS
😍 🙂 😐 ☹️ 😢

APPROX. HOURS _____

GET UP TIME: _____

TODAY I INTEND TO:
_____
_____
_____
_____

WATER INTAKE (OUNCES)
8 16 24 32
40 48 56 64

HOW AM I FEELING THIS EVENING?
😍 🙂 😐 ☹️ 😢

WHAT I ATE TODAY:

THREE THINGS THAT I AM GRATEFUL FOR:
_____
_____
_____

SELF CARE ACTIVITY OF THE DAY
_____
_____
_____

WHAT I MANAGED TO ACCOMPLISH TODAY || GO YOU!
_____
_____
_____

SOMETHING THAT MADE ME FEEL GOOD TODAY:

REFLECTIONS

BRAIN DUMP

A BRAIN DUMP IS A FREE-WRITING SESSION WHERE YOU UNLOAD ANYTHING ON YOUR MIND. USE THE SPACE BELOW TO WRITE OR DOODLE WHATEVER IS ON YOUR MIND IN THIS MOMENT. THE GOAL IS TO CLEAR SPACE IN YOUR BRAIN.

DAILY CHECK-IN REPORT

DATE: _____

MO TU WE TH FR SA SU

HOW AM I FEELING THIS MORNING?
- GREAT
- GOOD
- OKAY
- NOT GOOD
- AWFUL

MY SLEEP LAST NIGHT WAS

APPROX. HOURS _____

GET UP TIME: _____

TODAY I INTEND TO: _____
_____
_____
_____

WATER INTAKE (OUNCES)

8   16   24   32
40   48   56   64

HOW AM I FEELING THIS EVENING?

WHAT I ATE TODAY:

THREE THINGS THAT I AM GRATEFUL FOR:
_____
_____
_____

SELF CARE ACTIVITY OF THE DAY
_____
_____
_____

WHAT I MANAGED TO ACCOMPLISH TODAY || GO YOU!
_____
_____
_____

SOMETHING THAT MADE ME FEEL GOOD TODAY:

REFLECTIONS

BRAIN DUMP

A BRAIN DUMP IS A FREE-WRITING SESSION WHERE YOU UNLOAD ANYTHING ON YOUR MIND. USE THE SPACE BELOW TO WRITE OR DOODLE WHATEVER IS ON YOUR MIND IN THIS MOMENT. THE GOAL IS TO CLEAR SPACE IN YOUR BRAIN.

DAILY CHECK-IN REPORT

DATE: _____

MO TU WE TH FR SA SU

HOW AM I FEELING THIS MORNING?
- GREAT
- GOOD
- OKAY
- NOT GOOD
- AWFUL

MY SLEEP LAST NIGHT WAS

APPROX. HOURS _____

GET UP TIME: _____

TODAY I INTEND TO:
_____
_____
_____

WATER INTAKE (OUNCES)
8 16 24 32
40 48 56 64

HOW AM I FEELING THIS EVENING?

WHAT I ATE TODAY:

THREE THINGS THAT I AM GRATEFUL FOR:
_____
_____
_____

SELF CARE ACTIVITY OF THE DAY
_____
_____
_____

WHAT I MANAGED TO ACCOMPLISH TODAY || GO YOU!
_____
_____
_____

SOMETHING THAT MADE ME FEEL GOOD TODAY:

REFLECTIONS

BRAIN DUMP

A BRAIN DUMP IS A FREE-WRITING SESSION WHERE YOU UNLOAD ANYTHING ON YOUR MIND. USE THE SPACE BELOW TO WRITE OR DOODLE WHATEVER IS ON YOUR MIND IN THIS MOMENT. THE GOAL IS TO CLEAR SPACE IN YOUR BRAIN.

SAVE IT FOR THERAPY

Honest Thoughts Journal

SAVE IT FOR THERAPY

Affirmations for Fear

 I WAS MADE TO DO HARD THINGS.

 I AM BRAVE AND TRUST THE STEPS I AM TAKING.

 I AM ON A NEW PATH WHERE FEAR NO LONGER SERVES ME.

 I CHOOSE TO PUSH THROUGH EVEN WHEN I AM AFRAID.

 MY FEAR IS ALLOWED TO SHOW UP BUT IT IS NOT ALLOWED TO STAY.

SO WHAT'S ON YOUR MIND TODAY?

SO WHAT'S ON YOUR MIND TODAY?

SO WHAT'S ON YOUR MIND TODAY?

SO WHAT'S ON YOUR MIND TODAY?

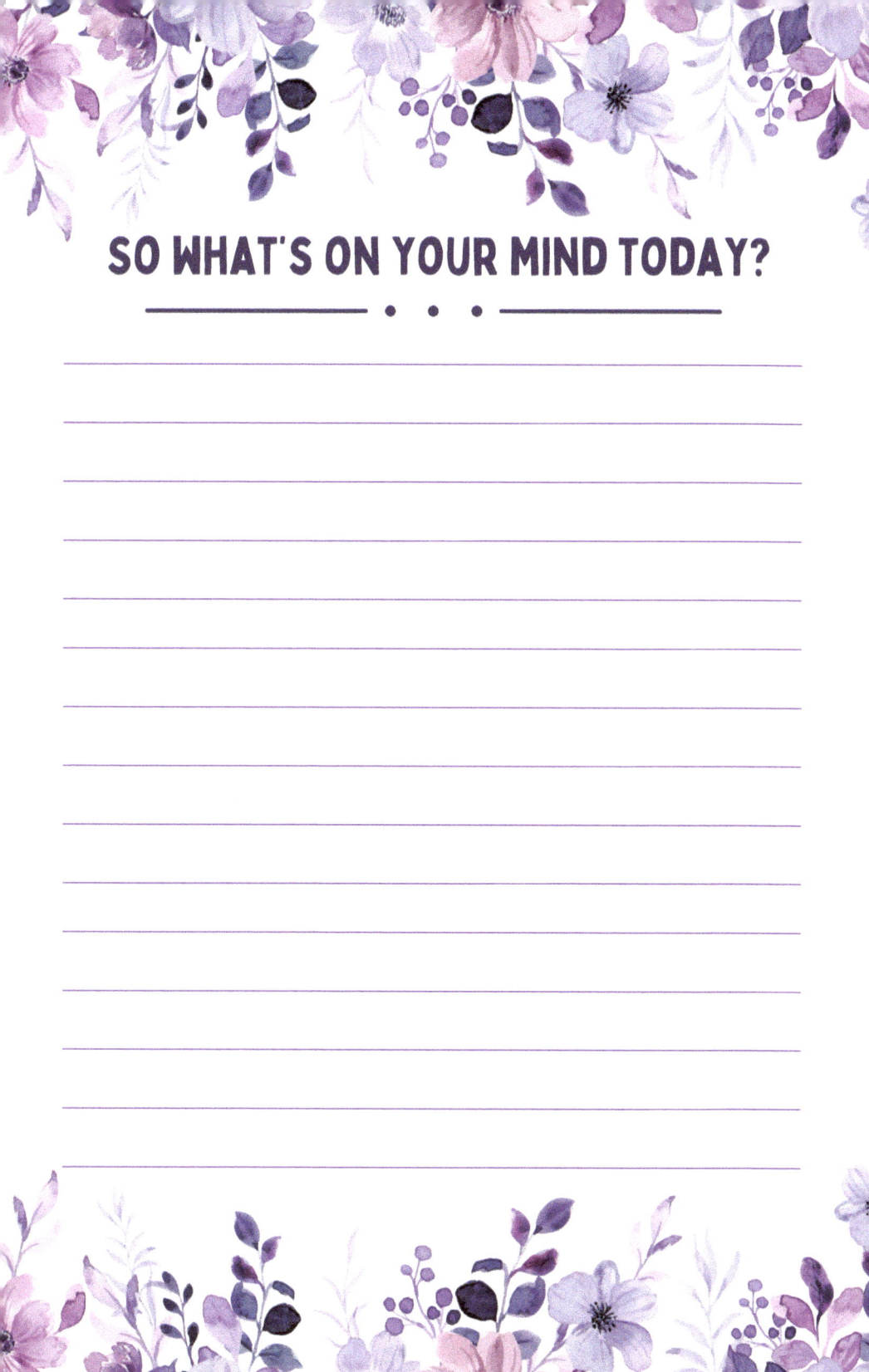

SO WHAT'S ON YOUR MIND TODAY?

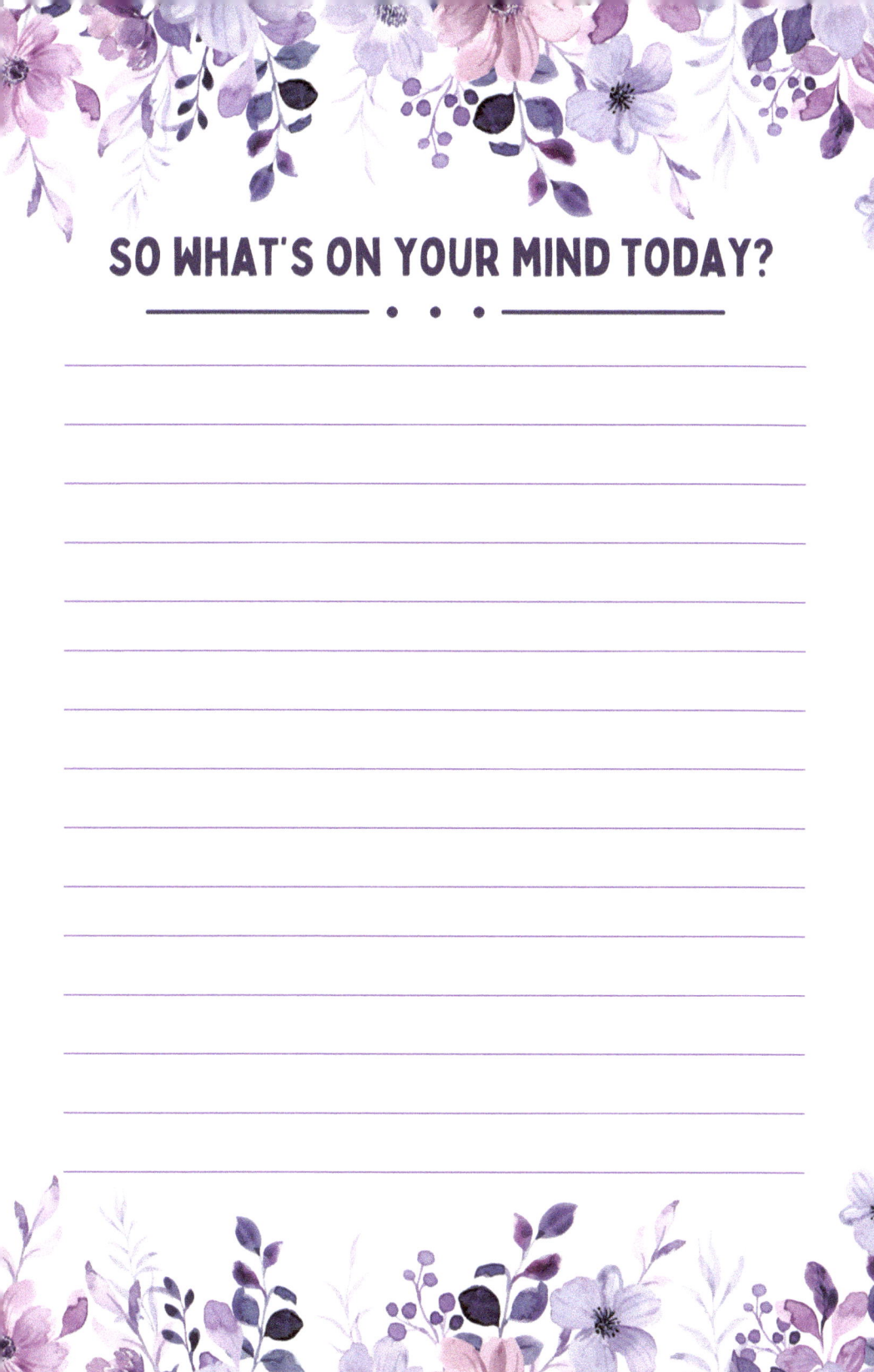
SO WHAT'S ON YOUR MIND TODAY?

SO WHAT'S ON YOUR MIND TODAY?

SO WHAT'S ON YOUR MIND TODAY?

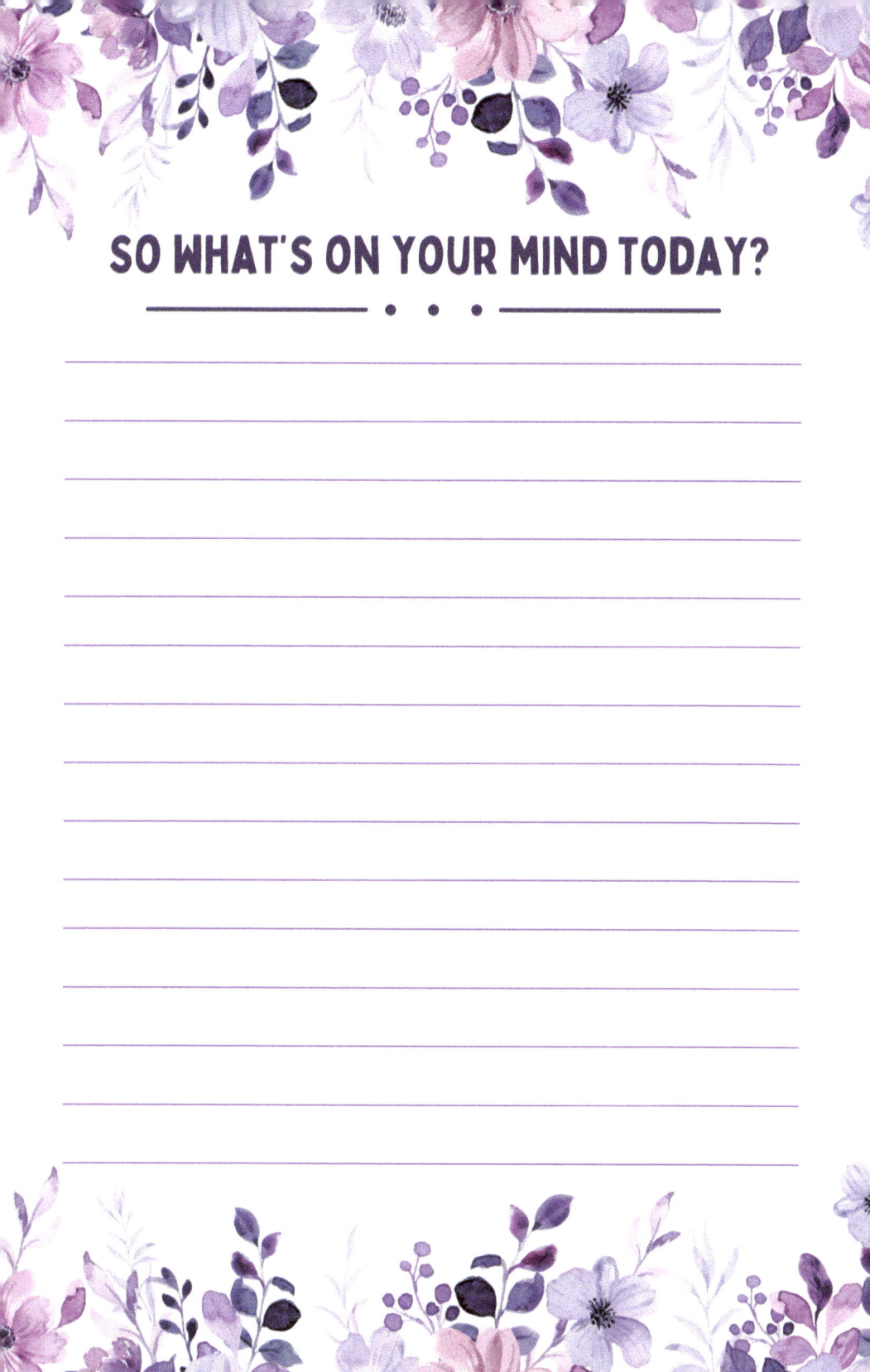
SO WHAT'S ON YOUR MIND TODAY?

SO WHAT'S ON YOUR MIND TODAY?

SO WHAT'S ON YOUR MIND TODAY?

SO WHAT'S ON YOUR MIND TODAY?

SO WHAT'S ON YOUR MIND TODAY?

SO WHAT'S ON YOUR MIND TODAY?

SO WHAT'S ON YOUR MIND TODAY?

SO WHAT'S ON YOUR MIND TODAY?

SO WHAT'S ON YOUR MIND TODAY?

www.ingramcontent.com/pod-product-compliance
Ingram Content Group UK Ltd.
Pitfield, Milton Keynes, MK11 3LW, UK
UKHW020239240426
12049UKWH00008B/133